Adjectives and Adverbs

© 2015 OnBoard Academics, Inc
Portsmouth, NH
800-596-3175
www.onboardacademics.com
ISBN: 978-1-63096-032-2

ALL RIGHTS RESERVED. This book contains material protected under International and Federal Copyright Laws and Treaties. Any unauthorized reprint or use of this material is prohibited. No part of this book may be reproduced or transmitted in any form or by any means, electronic or mechanical, including photocopying, reprinting, recording, or by any information storage and retrieval system without expressed written permission from the author / publisher.

OnBoard Academic's books are specifically designed to be used as printed workbooks or as on-screen instruction. Each page offers focused exercises and students quickly master topics with enough proficiency to move on to the next level.

OnBoard Academic's lessons are used in over 25,000 classrooms to rave reviews. Our lessons are aligned to the most recent governmental standards and are updated from time to time as standards change. Correlation documents are located on our website. Our lessons are created, edited and evaluated by educators to ensure top quality and real life success.

Interactive lessons for digital whiteboards, mobile devices, and PCs are available at www.onboardacademics.com. These interactive lessons make great additions to our books.

You can always reach us at customerservice@onboardacademics.com.

Adjectives

Key Vocabulary

adjectives

describing words

OnBoard Academics Workbook

K-2 ELA

Describe Javiér's hair.

Javiér has ☐ hair.

Long, black, spiky. What do we call these words?

What adjectives would you use to describe this dinosaur?

_____
_____
_____
_____
_____
_____

OnBoard Academics Workbook K-2 ELA

Dinosaur adjective word search.

```
a g h m i v e k d v
s g h u n g r y d x
u v u w l o i k d s
o r g t k d b n k c
i c e q u m i g o a
c k f e h o u r u r
o e s b l v y k d y
r n f d h o p g u t
e c k b k c i d o t
f c g f t b i y o t
```

big

huge

scary

ferocious

hungry

OnBoard Academics Workbook   K-2 ELA

Think of adjectives that help us to describe pigs.

1. They have ___ skin.

2. They often have ___ tails.

3. They have ___ snouts and ___ eyes.

_____

Think of adjectives that help us to describe sharks.

1. Most types are ___ in color.

2. They often have ___ teeth.

3. The Great White is a ___ type.

OnBoard Academics Workbook

K-2 ELA

Identify the adjectives.
Highlight or circle the adjectives in this text.

 Owen was excited. Today was his first day at a new school. He ate a large breakfast, grabbed his heavy backpack, and ran to catch the yellow school bus.

"Have a great day!" shouted his proud Mom and Dad.

Match the adjectives.
These adjectives are across from the wrong nouns. Draw a line to pair them with a noun that makes more sense.

adjective	noun
old	soda
smelly	nail
rusty	socks
cold	desk
tidy	painting

OnBoard Academics, Inc.   www.onboardacademics.com

5

OnBoard Academics Workbook   K-2 ELA

Name_____

Adjectives Quiz

1. An adjective is an action word. True or false?

2. I have a _____ pillow.
   a. fruity
   b. fast
   c. fluffy
   d. friendly

3. The table had a _____ leg.
   a. wobbly
   b. painful
   c. cheerful
   d. anxious

4. The sun was _____ yellow.
   a. dark
   b. bright
   c. little
   d. fluffy

5. The ballerina wore a _____ outfit.
   a. old
   b. slow
   c. fancy
   d. cold

Adverbs

Key Vocabulary

verb

adverb

OnBoard Academics Workbook Grade 3 ELA

What is an adverb?

> An adverb is a word that describes a verb. They are words that tell us how, when or where something happens.

Read the passage below. Underneath each adverb (in red) indicate if the adverb tells us how, when or where?

Owen quickly tied his sneakers.

The big basketball game is today.

His teammates waited nearby.

©2013 OnBoard Academics, Inc.   www.onboardacademics.com

OnBoard Academics Workbook

Grade 3 ELA

Some adverbs tell how action happens.

> Adverbs that tell **how** usually end **-ly**.

Circle the words that tell how action happens in the passage below.

Alison's horse trotted beautifully.

She easily won the blue ribbon.

_____

Using the suggestions below, describe how the girl is running.

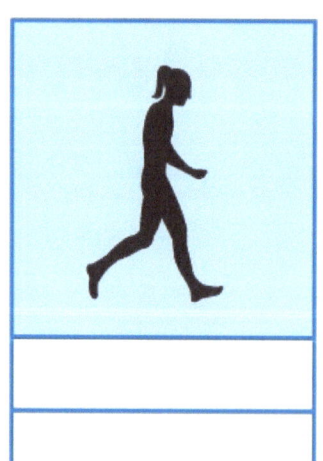 

| steadily | loudly | quickly | angrily |
| rapidly | softly | playfully | slowly |

©2013 OnBoard Academics, Inc.   www.onboardacademics.com

OnBoard Academics Workbook — Grade 3 ELA

Some adverbs tell when an action happens.
Read the passage below and notice the adverbs that tell us when something happens.

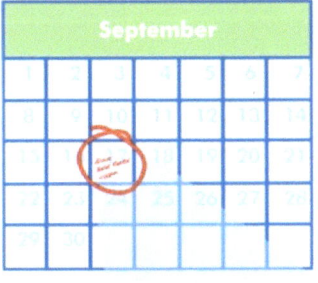

Hey Susan,
I have my ballet recital *today*! I am very excited, and a little nervous. We have to leave *soon*, but I will grab a quick snack before we go. *Tomorrow* I start tap dance lessons!

— Alison

Put a check mark next to the sentence if it has an adverb that tells us when an action happens and an X if it does not have an adverb that tells when.

1. My family drove to the zoo yesterday.
2. We ate lunch by the monkeys.
3. The elephants were boring.
4. I will visit the penguins next.
5. Soon the polar bears will wake up.
6. I will go to the aquarium tomorrow.

OnBoard Academics Workbook — Grade 3 ELA

Adverbs also tell us where an action happened.
Read the passage below and notice the adverbs that tell us where an action happens.

Owen's Dad drove **around**.

There were parking spots **everywhere**.

Word Search
Find the adverbs and circle them.

e	g	h	m	y	b	r	a	e	n
v	g	f	o	r	h	h	m	d	a
e	v	o	e	a	e	e	e	d	t
r	a	u	t	a	d	b	a	k	t
y	r	r	d	m	w	a	t	h	f
w	o	a	e	f	l	a	e	u	r
h	u	s	e	r	v	r	y	d	y
e	n	d	o	h	e	p	g	u	t
r	d	o	b	k	h	e	r	e	t
e	p	g	f	t	s	r	p	k	t

ahead

around

away

here

everywhere

nearby

there

©2013 OnBoard Academics, Inc.   www.onboardacademics.com

Match how, when or where to describe the adverb.

☐ **Yesterday** Ben was painting his room.

☐ The telephone rang **loudly**.

☐ Ben ran **downstairs** to answer it.

☐ He **accidentally** knocked over the paint can.

☐ The paint spilled **everywhere**!

| how | when | where |

Circle the adverb in each sentence.

 Did you know that cheetahs used to live here?

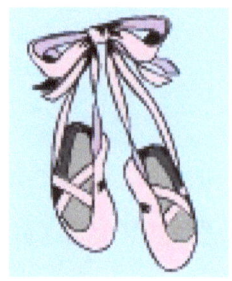 The ballerina pirouetted gracefully.

 Owen ran outside to play.

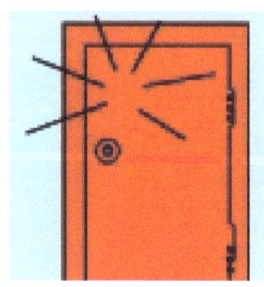 The police officer knocked on the door loudly.

OnBoard Academics Workbook

Grade 3 ELA

Use each word in a sentence . Write your sentence below.

gently

soon

nearby

Name_____

Adverb Quiz

1. True or false? Adverbs describe nouns

2. Circle the adverb in this sentence. I stepped softly on the grass.

3. Circle the adverb in this sentence. He washes the windows first.

4. Fill in the blank with an adverb. The athlete ran _____.

5. Fill in the blank with an adverb describing how. The lighs shone _____.

6. Fill in the blank with an adverb describing where. When is started raining we ran _____

7. Fill in the blank with and adverb describing when. We watched fireworks _____.

8. Circle the sentence that does not have an adverb.
   a. The team anxiously approached the stadium.
   b. The book had a simple green cover.
   c. Mia neatly wrote her name.
   d. The bus stop is nearby.

©2013 OnBoard Academics, Inc.   www.onboardacademics.com

OnBoard Academics Workbook

Grade 4 ELA

Adjectives and Adverbs

Key Vocabulary

adjective

adverb

Adjectives and Adverbs

> Adjectives and adverbs add descriptive detail to a sentence; *adjectives* describe *nouns* or *pronouns*, and *adverbs* describe *verbs, adjectives* or other *adverbs*.

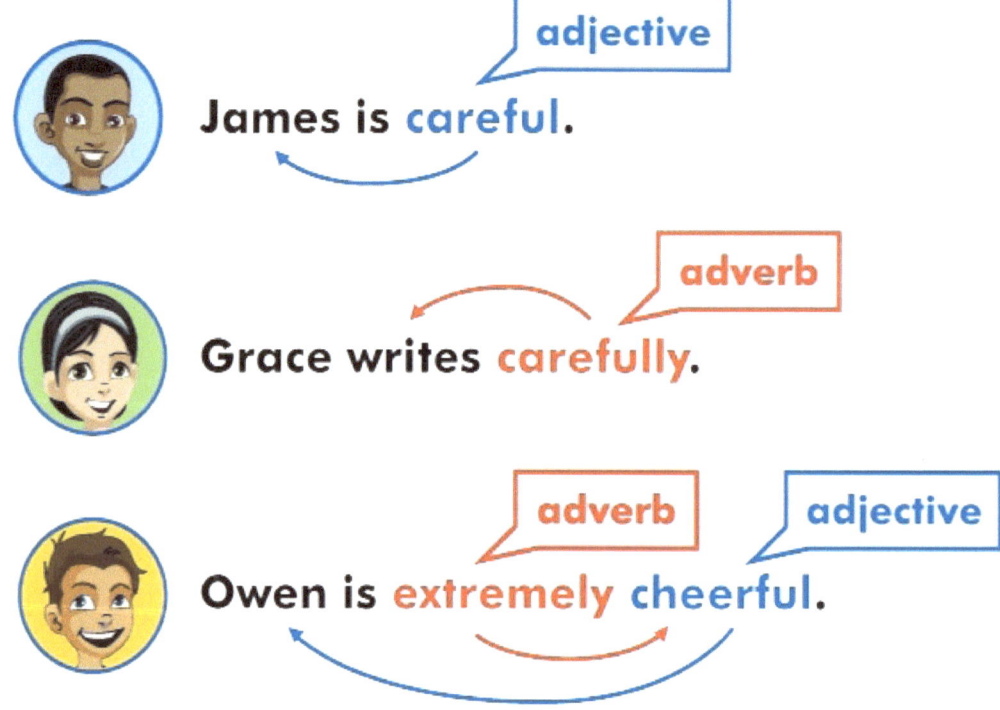

OnBoard Academics Workbook — Grade 4 ELA

Adjectives and Nouns

Write in a sensible adjective from the list provided for each noun.

	adjective	noun
complex		rabbit
violent		riddle
messy		game
exciting		soup
hot		bedroom
quick		storm

Adverbs

Adverbs can tell us how, when or where an action happens.

adverb describing how
Fernando quickly brushed his teeth.

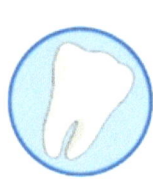
adverb describing when
Today he is going to the dentist.

adverb describing where
His mom waited in the car outside.

OnBoard Academics Workbook — Grade 4 ELA

How, When or Where

Complete the sentence with a how, when or where adverb.

| Jenna came ____ to my house ____. |
| She knocked ____ on the door when she arrived. |
| We played ____ ____ most of the day. |
| She ____ left at 3, but she'll be back ____. |

how	where	when
rapidly loudly reluctantly safely	outside often yesterday next	later around ahead over

---

Underline the adverb. Circle what the adverb modifies. Label the box with the part of speech that has been modified.

☐ Alison barely won the 100 meter dash.

☐ She will compete in the long jump next.

☐ Her parents were watching nearby.

☐ They were really proud.

☐ Alison won the long jump quite easily.

verb   **adjective**   **adverb**

Sort the adjectives and adverbs.

The adorable kitten batted at the yarn.

Mia ran outside to see her Dad's new car.

The black dog barked viciously at the postman.

Snails are slimy and move very slowly.

adjective	adverb

Hint

Many adverbs end with -ly.

OnBoard Academics Workbook — Grade 4 ELA

Summary of Adjectives and Adverbs

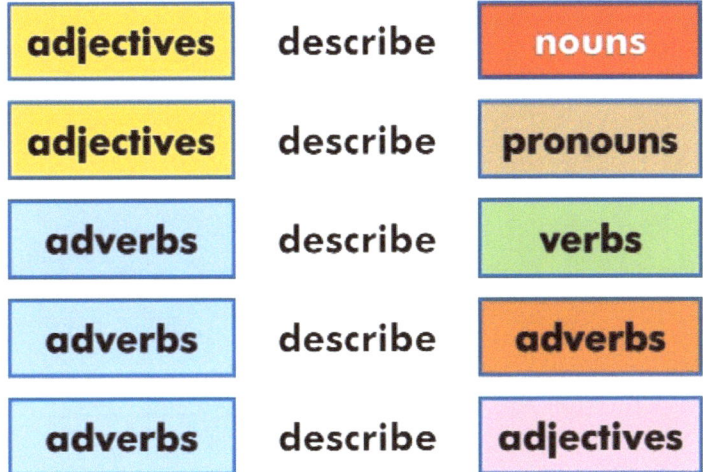

Compare the color coded words in the paragraph below with the guide above.

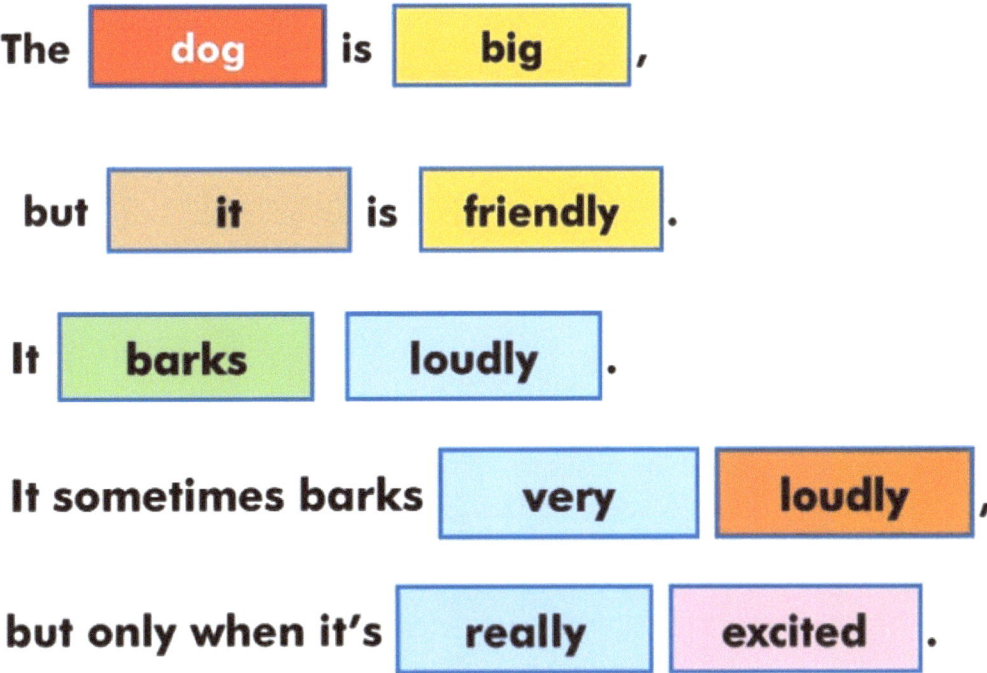

Fill in the blanks.
If you have colors, make the adjectives red and the adverbs blue. If not, circle the adjectives.

Alison and Grace went on a _____ hike in the woods. "We'll have to eat_____," Alison said. "I can _____ walk I am _____ hungry!" The girls threw down their _____ backpacks and ate their sandwiches _____ly. "This is the _____ sandwich I have ever had!" Alison cried. It's _____!"

OnBoard Academics Workbook — Grade 4 ELA

Adjectives and Adverbs Quiz

1. An adverb modifies a verb, adjective or other adverb and tells how, why or when. True or false?

2. Identify the adjective: I was out of breath as I climbed up the giant hill.
    a. breath
    b. climbed
    c. giant
    d. hill

3. Which sentence does not have an adverb?
    a. I silently crept down the spooky path.
    b. The dog happily ran after the blue ball.
    c. The duckling was over near the pond.
    d. The kitchen floor was covered with flour.

4. The scientist _____ studied the insects.
    a. lazily
    b. carefully
    c. loudly
    d. colorfully

5. My _____ stomach rumbled
    a. smart
    b. right
    c. busy
    d. empty

OnBoard Academics, Inc.   www.onboardacademics.com

www.ingramcontent.com/pod-product-compliance
Lightning Source LLC
LaVergne TN
LVHW071031070426
835507LV00002B/114